EJAGHAM

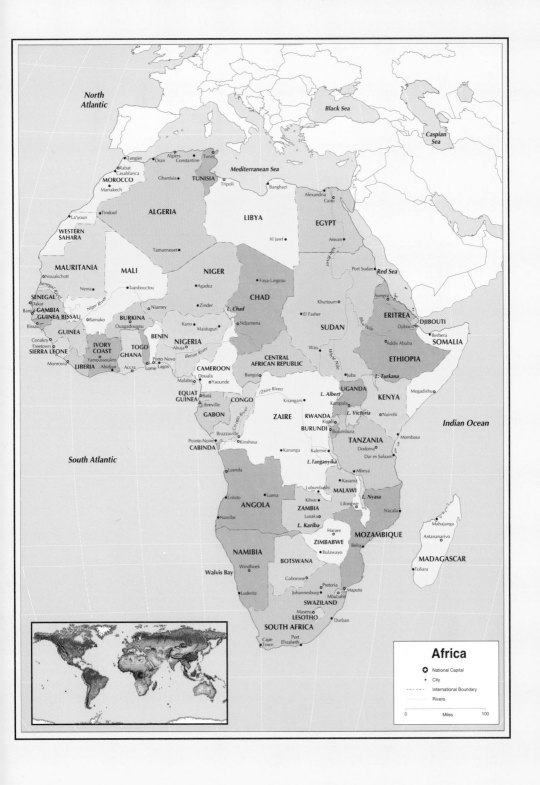

North
Atlantic

Black Sea

Caspian
Sea

Tangier
Algiers
Oran   Constantine   Tunis
Rabat
Casablanca
MOROCCO   Ghardaia   TUNISIA
Marrakech   Tripoli   Mediterranean Sea
                                                              Banghazi   Alexandria
La'youn   Tindouf   Cairo
WESTERN   ALGERIA   LIBYA   EGYPT
SAHARA
                                            Al Jawf   Aswan
MAURITANIA   MALI   Tamanrasset   Port Sudan Red Sea
Nouakchott   NIGER   Asmera
             Nema   Agadez   Faya-Largeau   DJIBOUTI
Senegal River   Tombouctou   CHAD   Khartoum   ERITREA Djibouti
SENEGAL   Niger River Zinder   L. Chad   Berbera
Dakar   Niamey   Ndjamena   El Fasher   SOMALIA
Banjul GAMBIA   Bamako Kano Maiduguri   Addis Ababa
GUINEA BISSAU   BURKINA   SUDAN
Bissau   GUINEA   Ouagadougou   Wau   White Nile   ETHIOPIA
Conakry   BENIN   Blue Nile
Freetown IVORY TOGO NIGERIA   Benue River   CENTRAL   Juba   L. Turkana
SIERRA LEONE   COAST GHANA   Abuja Porto Novo AFRICAN REPUBLIC
Monrovia Yamoussoukro Accra Lome Lagos   Bangui   UGANDA   KENYA
LIBERIA   Abidjan   CAMEROON   L. Albert   Mogadishu
                   Malabo   Douala   Kisangani Kampala
              EQUAT. Bata Yaounde   (Zaire River)   L. Victoria Nairobi
              GUINEA Libreville CONGO   RWANDA
                     GABON   ZAIRE   Kigali   Mombasa
                              Congo River   BURUNDI Bujumbura
              Pointe-Noire Brazzaville   TANZANIA
                     CABINDA Kinshasa   Kananga Kalemie Dodoma
                                                    Dar es Salaam
                              Luanda   L. Tanganyika Mbeya
South Atlantic   Kasama
                    Lobito Luena   Lubumbashi MALAWI L. Nyasa
                    ANGOLA   ZAMBIA   Kitwe Lilongwe   Nacala
                    Namibe   Lusaka
                                 L. Kariba   Harare   MOZAMBIQUE   Mahajanga
                    NAMIBIA   BOTSWANA ZIMBABWE Bulawayo Beira   Antananarivo
                                                                    MADAGASCAR
                    Walvis Bay   Windhoek   Toliara
                              Gaborone   Pretoria
                    Luderitz   Johannesburg Maputo
                                      Mbabane   SWAZILAND
                              SOUTH AFRICA Maseru LESOTHO
                                      Cape Port   Durban
                                      Town Elizabeth

Indian Ocean

Africa

⊕ National Capital
• City
- - - International Boundary
—— Rivers

0   Miles   100

The Heritage Library of African Peoples

EJAGHAM

Ute Röschenthaler, Ph.D.

THE ROSEN PUBLISHING GROUP, INC.
NEW YORK

This book is dedicated to the Ejagham people who did their best to teach me about their culture. Choosing the contents was not easy but selecting the pictures was even more difficult. I hope those who do and those who do not find their contributions in here will accept it that way. One major aim of this book is to give the Ejagham youth a feeling for the importance of their cultural heritage.

Published in 1996 by The Rosen Publishing Group, Inc.
29 East 21st Street, New York, NY 10010

First Edition

Manufactured in the United States of America

Library of Congress Cataloging-in-Publication Data

Röschenthaler, Ute.
    Ejagham / Ute Röschenthaler. — 1st ed.
        p.   cm. — (The heritage library of African peoples)
    Includes bibliographical references and index.
    Summary: A look at the culture, history, and contemporary life of
the Ejagham people of the Cross River area of Cameroon and Nigeria.
    ISBN 0-8239-1993-5
    1. Ejagham (African people)—Juvenile literature. [1. Ejagham
(African people) 2. Africa—Social life and customs.] I. Title.
II. Series.
DT571.E35R67   1996
966.9—dc20   96-12298
                                                                        CIP
                                                                        AC

Contents

INTRODUCTION

THERE IS EVERY REASON FOR US TO KNOW something about Africa and to understand its past and the way of life of its peoples. Africa is a rich continent that has for centuries provided the world with art, culture, labor, wealth, and natural resources. It has vast mineral deposits, fossil fuels, and commercial crops.

But perhaps most important is the fact that fossil evidence indicates that human beings originated in Africa. The earliest traces of human beings and their tools are almost two million years old. Their descendants have migrated throughout the world. To be human is to be of African descent.

The experiences of the peoples who stayed in Africa are as rich and as diverse as of those who established themselves elsewhere. This series of books describes their environment, their modes of subsistence, their relationships, and their customs and beliefs. The books present the variety of languages, histories, cultures, and religions that are to be found on the African continent. They demonstrate the historical linkages between African peoples and the way contemporary Africa has been affected by European colonial rule.

Africa is large, complex, and diverse. It encompasses an area of more than 11,700,000 square miles. The United States, Europe, and India could fit easily into it. The sheer size is an indication of the continent's great variety in geography, terrain, climate, flora, fauna, peoples, languages, and cultures.

Much of contemporary Africa has been shaped by European colonial rule, industrialization, urbanization, and the demands of a world economic system. For more than seventy years, large regions of Africa were ruled by Great Britain, France, Belgium, Portugal, and Spain. African peoples from various ethnic, linguistic, and cultural backgrounds were brought together to form colonial states.

For decades Africans struggled to gain their independence. It was not until after World War II that the colonial territories became independent African states. Today, almost all of Africa is ruled by Africans. Large numbers of Africans live in modern cities. Rural Africa is also being transformed, and yet its people still engage in many of their customs and beliefs.

Contemporary circumstances and natural events have not always been kind to ordinary Africans. Today, however, new popular social movements and technological innovations pose great promise for future development.

George C. Bond, Ph.D., Director
Institute of African Studies
Columbia University, New York

The Ejagham are famous for their wooden sculptures and their skin-covered masks. Here, a member of a women's club dances with a brightly painted wooden sculpture upon her head.

1

THE LAND AND
THE PEOPLE

"WHEREVER YOU HAVE A FRIEND OR A
relative you have a place to stay." This Ejagham
proverb conveys the hospitality of the Ejagham
people. It also implies that to visit a person is to
pay respect to him or her. Therefore, men and
women, youths and adults, travel a lot. Elderly
and respected people are more likely to stay at
home, expecting to receive visitors. There is
always a reason to visit another village or town
to see relatives or friends, buy goods, arrange
affairs, or attend festivities.

Many Ejagham live in towns and cities today,
but their traditional home is the Cross River
area of southwestern Cameroon and southeast-
ern Nigeria.

Cameroon and Nigeria each have more than
one hundred ethnic groups, each with its own
language. The language of the Ejagham is called

The Cross River is an important transportation route for the Ejagham.
Above, a group of Ejagham travels along the river in a canoe.

Ejagham, as the people call themselves. They are
also known by their neighbors as the Ekoi.

The large Cross River area is hilly and thinly
populated. It is covered by a thick rain forest
and drained by many rivers and creeks. The
largest river is the Cross River. It curves from
the Cameroon grasslands to the Atlantic Ocean.
Ejagham territory is concentrated within the
large southwest bend of the Cross River.

Along with the Ejagham, many other small
ethnic groups live in the area. The Banyang live
near the river's source at the foot of the moun-
tains of the Cameroon grasslands. The Boki and
the Igbo occupy the northwestern bank of the
Cross River. The Efik live at Calabar in Nigeria,
where the Cross River enters the Atlantic Ocean.

▼ THE VILLAGE ▼

The Ejagham live in about 150 villages and small towns, which are connected by roads or foot paths. Usually a few coconut trees indicate the vicinity of a village. A huge silkcotton or *mboma* tree may stand at the entrance of a village or in its center.

At the village center is the community hall where meetings take place. Behind it are the *njom*, the charms to protect the village against thieves and people with bad intentions, such as witches and sorcerers.

The houses are built along the main road, with small gardens behind them. Many trees are grown: oil palms and banana, mango, papaya, and orange trees.

Each village, *etek*, is built near a river or stream for an easy water supply. Around the villages are the fields where the women grow the food crops such as yams, cassava, banana, sweet potato, corn, and other vegetables.

Beyond the fields the forest starts. Many species of animals live in the forest, including elephants, leopards, rhinos, crocodiles, pythons, antelopes, and monkeys. It is regarded as something very special to catch one of the big animals. Among their neighbors the Ejagham have a good reputation as hunters. Today hunting has been reduced because laws protect animals.

Today the Ejagham live both in large cities and towns and in small, traditional villages. Seen here are two Ejagham villages in Cameroon.

▼ THE ANNUAL CYCLE ▼

The year is dominated by the rainy season, from April to September, and the dry season, from October to March. Because of the heavy rainfall, the climate is extremely humid.

During the rainy season, rain falls continually every day. Most of the work in the fields is done in this season. In March, men and women prepare the fields for planting in April as soon as the first rains start to fall. They plant most of the grain left from the previous harvest, but keep some back so that the family has food until the next harvest is ready.

Everything grows fast in this climate, so to weed and care for the fields means much work. Thus the rainy season is a busy time. It is a hard season as well, because there is little food to eat once most of the seed grain has been planted. Women do the main work on the fields.

Usually the harvest is ready in September when the rains stop. The Ejagham store some of the crops in small houses alongside the fields; the rest they carry to the village. There is always a harvest ceremony at which the village chief makes a thanksgiving sacrifice and offers part of the crops to God and the ancestors. Some villages conclude the offering with a big dance festival.

In the dry season, rain is only occasional. Especially in November and December, the time

The dry season after the Ejagham harvest is the time for many social activities. Here, villagers gather for one of the dry season's many feasts and celebrations.

of the harmattan (a dusty, dry wind from the Sahara Desert), sudden, heavy thunderstorms occur. The dry season is the time for social activities in the villages. Since the people go only rarely to the fields, they spend much time visiting friends and making arts and crafts. After the harvest there is plenty of food to celebrate the major festivities. The Ejagham are also famous for their many dances and masquerades. Each village has several clubs that own masks. Various clubs are invited to dance at the numerous celebrations.▲

chapter

2
HISTORY

WE CAN BE CERTAIN THAT THE EJAGHAM have a long history, because there is no society without historical change. But there are no written accounts of Ejagham history, so we have to rely on Ejagham oral accounts. Oral tradition includes both historical and mythical events. Myths are considered even more important than historical accounts. Myths contain the essence of events, whereas history merely provides the facts. Lake Ejagham, lying in the heart of the Ejagham country, plays an important role as a mythical place of origin and power.

▼ VILLAGE HISTORY ▼

The one historical event that every Ejagham person regards as most important is the founding of their village. Some villages have a long history and occupied several places before they

THE MYSTERIOUS LAKE

Once there was a hunter who came from a faraway land. At the end of an unsuccessful day he found his way to a small, round lake. Some call it Lake Ejagham, others Ejengeleng Ayip, which means "water producing round waves." It lies in the heart of Ejagham country. Everybody approaches this lake respectfully and nobody hunts near by for fear of angering the guardians of the lake, who might send misfortune and illness. It is said that whoever bathes in the lake will be drawn down into the center of the earth by a whirlpool.

Lake Ejagham is guarded by spirits. White eagles circle in the air, rare fish live in the lake, and great pythons inhabit the shores. In the water resides a legendary python called Mbogonemandem, who keeps a beautiful, shining jewel in her mouth. When she glides out of the water in the evening, she takes it out of her mouth to light her way when searching for food.

While resting, the tired and hungry hunter suddenly discovered plates full of delicious food on the bank. First he was scared, but since he was hungry and nobody else appeared, he decided to eat it. He then continued his journey and reached the nearby village. He told the amazed inhabitants of the food that had miraculously appeared. The people liked the hunter, so he married a girl and remained in the village. Later, other people also found gifts of food from the ancestors delivered by the spirits to the shores of the lake. So it is that people make offerings to the spirits and ancestors who continue to support them in difficult times.

came to their present site. Migrations of families or entire villages are often motivated by disputes or by natural disasters, such as persistent crop failure, childlessness of several families, or drought.

People feel very strongly connected to the places where they live. They revere the earth that produces the crops and in which the deceased are buried. Similarly, they respect the river from which they take their water and the animals surrounding them in the forest. Thus the founder of a village is very important, because the well-being of the entire community depends on his choice of the site. He and his mother are honored by name whenever something special happens and offerings for the ancestors are made. Every chief of the village and important elder since the founding of the village is similarly remembered.

▼ WARS AND TRADERS ▼

In former centuries the Ejagham were famous as skilled and brave warriors. They lived at peace with most of the neighboring villages and ethnic groups. Nevertheless, they waged wars with others. The Ejagham owned effective war charms with which they could confuse or hypnotize their enemies. As a war strategy, for example, they utilized scarecrows like giant puppets, with strings attached. They placed these on the

The Ejagham are famous for their art forms. They maintained their traditional arts throughout the colonial period and still practice them today. Seen here is an Ejagham dancer with a painted mask.

battlefront and hid nearby. By jiggling the strings, the Ejagham made the scarecrows seem alive. These became the enemy's targets. While the enemy shot at the fake figures, which never fell, the Ejagham warriors crawled toward the enemies and finally captured them.

The Ejagham also came into contact with more distant people, including Igbo traders from the western bank of the Cross River and the Hausa, who traveled to Ejagham country from as far north as the Sahara to sell their trading goods. From the 1500s on, the Ejagham had to confront slave traders from the Atlantic coast, who invaded the country in search of captives.

▼ COLONIZATION AND INDEPENDENCE ▼

At the turn of the twentieth century the first Europeans settled in Ejagham country. They were competing British and German missionaries and colonial officers. Since they did not know Ejagham country well, they drew a borderline through the territory to divide it between the British and the Germans. The British part was called Nigeria and the German part Cameroon. The Ejagham strongly opposed the colonial officers, whom they recognized as hostile invaders. Although their opposition was successful for some time, the Ejagham were forced to surrender in the end.

The Germans occupied Cameroon only for

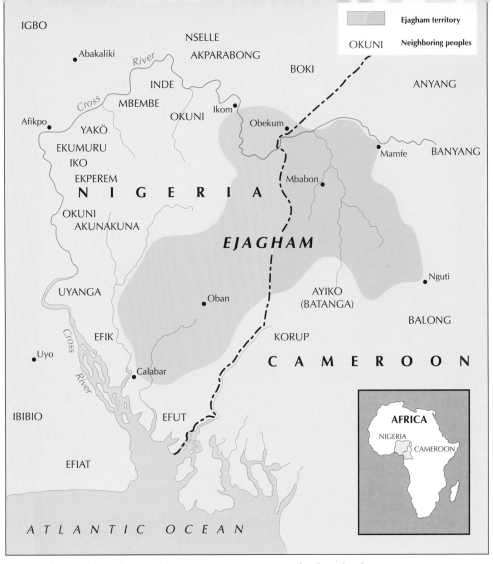

The Ejagham live in the Cross River area on the border between Nigeria and Cameroon.

about twenty years, because after their defeat in World War I in 1918 they were forced to surrender their colonies. As a result, Cameroon was divided into two: one part for the British, and the other for the French. The Ejagham country fell into the British part and therefore was reunited with the other Ejagham land already under British colonial rule.

British occupation lasted for about forty years. One of the major effects of British rule was the introduction of a warrant chief system. This meant that the British appointed chiefs to replace the villages' own chiefs. This "indirect rule," as it was known, was designed to enable the British to control the people more easily through the puppet chiefs. It resulted, however, in serious disputes over authority between the village chiefs and the warrant chiefs. These disputes continue to endanger the peace of Ejagham communities.

In 1960, Cameroon and Nigeria became independent. As a result, the part of Ejagham country that was formerly ruled by the Germans became part of Cameroon again in 1961. So today Ejagham territory is once again cut in half by a boundary that the Ejagham played no part in creating. This division causes inconveniences in daily life. If you visit relatives in an Ejagham village that is situated in the other state, you need different money. Ejagham people today have to know the different laws and regulations of the two countries. However, since Ejagham country lies at the outer regions of both Nigeria and Cameroon, the administrations do not interfere heavily in daily affairs. At the same time, neither administration has bothered to develop the region, and the Ejagham suffer from this neglect.▲

chapter

3

POLITICS AND SOCIETY

THE FAMILY PLAYS A VERY IMPORTANT ROLE in Ejagham society. The Ejagham are a patrilineal society: All those who have a common father, a grandfather, or a great-grandfather on the father's side are regarded as a family. Usually such an extended family is very large, often comprising up to a hundred people. The oldest man is regarded as the family head and, together with the family's oldest woman, makes the offerings to the ancestors; that is, to all the grandfathers and -mothers who lived before them.

▼ THE EXTENDED FAMILY ▼

All members of the same generation of this large family call each other "sisters" and "brothers." They call the older generation "mothers" and "fathers," and the young ones "children."

The Ejagham compare an extended family to

The family plays a very important role in Ejagham society. Above, an Ejagham family stands in front of their house, where most social activities take place.

a large tree with many branches. For a large family you also need a large house or compound. An extended family is thus called *ndebe-nju*, which means literally the branches (*ndebe*) of the house (*nju*).

In patrilineal societies like the Ejagham, a man's mother and wife, or wives, live with him, but they never really belong to his *ndebe-nju* or family, since they always belong to their own father's family.

Each "branch of the house," that is, each married man, lives in his own house. Such a house consists of the salon, where guests are received, and the kitchens and sleeping rooms for each of the wives and their children. The more wives a man can afford to marry, the

23

larger the house has to be. In addition, there must be rooms for older relatives and guest rooms for visiting relatives. The rooms are small, but since the climate is warm, most of the social activities take place outside under the large roof in front of the house. In fact, the Ejagham use the house mainly to sleep and to store their possessions.

Family members can expect mutual help and support from each other. To a large extent they share the daily activities and the family's possessions. They also support each other in difficult situations, since the entire family is regarded responsible for everything a member does. There is a strong hierarchy of age. Younger family members must obey the older ones. A younger brother will follow his older brother, even if the difference of age is only one year.

A husband must provide each of his wives with enough land for them to grow the food to feed the family throughout the year. The village's land is owned by the families. The family elders distribute the land among the married men, who in turn divide it among their wives, but keep some to plant their own cash crops.

▼ CLUBS ▼

Apart from belonging to a family, most Ejagham are members of one or more of the village's clubs or associations. They join a club,

Most Ejagham are members of a social club or association, such as a traditional village club or a social club within a modern city. Seen here are singers and dancers from an Ejagham village club.

okum, with their friends and agemates. Every village has several clubs for children, for men, for women, and for mixed membership. In fact, to be a respected person in the village, it is necessary to belong to an important club.

Each club has its own meeting room and a set of rules to which all the members agree to adhere. At a club meeting only members may take part. Most clubs have regular meetings at which important matters are discussed.

Depending on the aims of the club, the members help each other at their work and in difficult times, or they practice dancing. Often they eat and drink together and sing the club's songs. At festivities they bring out their masks for a

EJAGHAM PROVERBS

Nju aká énop,
nkok cáng ko.

When the house is not nice,
the fowl will not lay an egg.

Nkúé se, mme nnyû
cáng,
ntángá acot ekem a?

The wise tortoise said: I have no
hair on my head,
who am I to discuss matters
about cutting hair?

Mmon á fup ogbo,
á bhó mengé ejen.

If a child fears falling,
it will never learn to walk.

Ngbe se, ,,Ejûm cáng ka
ofang,
é rî ka osoná-mbéngé.''

The leopard says: ,,There is
nothing in being large,
what matters is being brave.''

Kpe oyimî o kêt,
ebhan a re ejâ.

Though you do your best,
someone will always criticize
you.

O kâ rê, â bh'p sik
nne esup.

The person who encourages you
to make trouble will not
accompany you to court.

Nkok á bhó cep ka
aji amê.

A hen, however small, has the
last word concerning her own
eggs.

Oghímme ka njem njok,
owóng mfúmé ya nyo.

Why not climb on the back
of an elephant to be able to pick
the fruits of a tree with your
mouth [easily].

dance. To become a member of a club you have to apply to the heads of the club. They decide whether you will be admitted and what your entrance fee will be. The new member is welcomed by a ceremony. It is not possible to leave a club; you remain a member for life.

The more important clubs have several grades and powerful secrets that may never be revealed to a nonmember. Clubs that possess secrets are very expensive to enter, but the extended family will usually help a relative raise the entrance fee.

▼ POLITICS ▼

A village may comprise several large families. It is governed by a council of elders, consisting of the oldest living members of each of the families. The elders are responsible for politics, make decisions and laws, and judge cases. They are very wise, are experts in using proverbs, and know everything that is going on in the village. One of them is the village chief, *ntuifam etek*. He is the ritual head of the community and of the clubs, but he has no political power of his own.

Some of the important clubs with secrets own masked dancers who help the elders in governing the village. The masked dancers are instructed by the elders to enforce laws and punish severe criminals. They then run around the village with whips, and all nonmembers hide in

their houses until the masks have done their
duty.

▼ TRIALS ▼

An attempt is first made to settle all disputes
within the family or among the families
concerned. If no satisfactory agreement
can be negotiated, the case is taken to
the village council of elders. Today a
matter can also be brought
before the civil court, but
usually this does not become
necessary.

The elders hear all the
parties involved, listen to
every opinion, and finally
decide the case. The person
found to be in the wrong is
usually fined a sum of money
or a quantity of goods. At the
very least, a drink offering to
honor the ancestors is
required as a fine. After the
verdict, the ancestors are informed
of the event, asked to forgive the
troublemaker, and invited to take part
in the drinking.

Today the Ejagham live under a modern legal system.
Some village disputes are still settled by swearing in front
of sacred charms, called *njom*. Above, the owner of a
njom holds the charm up for villagers to swear upon.

If the guilty person had tried to kill somebody, an owner of a *njom* must be called. The
guilty person must swear in front of the *njom*
that he or she will never do such a thing again.
It is understood that if anyone lies to a *njom*, the
njom will pursue that person and kill him or
her. Water is thrown over the hands of the guilty
person to wash away all bad intentions and
influences. Then the dispute is settled
and everybody disperses.▲

Njom come in many different forms and styles. The *njom* seen here
hangs in a traditional shrine.

In Ejagham villages, women spend the cool mornings preparing food for the main meal, which takes place in the hot afternoon. Here a young wife uses a pestle and mortar to crush food for the afternoon meal.

chapter

4

DAILY LIFE

DAILY ACTIVITIES START EARLY IN THE morning. At dawn, when the cry of the guinea fowl is heard, men and women rise to get the major work done before noon, because it usually becomes very hot during the day.

A man may participate in a club meeting or work on his banana, coffee, or cocoa plantation. Coffee and cocoa are so-called cash crops since they are sold overseas.

While the older children go to school, younger ones accompany their mother to the fields. She is eager to see that they are intact, since the animals of the bush may have destroyed the crops, the entire food for the family. A woman then decides which crops she will take home to prepare in the afternoon. In the afternoon, the schoolchildren generally help their mother take crops back to the village, col-

THE TALE OF THE FLY

Once a fly flew by a river in the forest. There she saw a fat python lying on the bank, baking herself in the sun. She remembered that pythons live beneath the waters in glittering palaces filled with riches.

The fly settled beside the snake and said, "I wish you would die so that I could have all your riches!" The python disliked the company of this fly and slithered down a nearby hole. It was the home of a hamster rat. The hamster rat offered his visitor a drink, and the python downed it along with the cup. The snake said she was hungry. The hamster rat gave her some food, which she swallowed together with the plate. The hamster rat feared that she might devour him next. He fled toward the monkey's place.

When the monkey saw the half-bald head of the white hamster-rat, he mistook it for a ghost from the village of the dead and fled up to the very top of a tree. In his panic he dislodged a coconut that fell right onto the trunk of an elephant, its most sensitive part. In agony, the elephant toppled a towering termite's nest, which smashed the egg of a guinea fowl. The mourning guinea fowl stopped announcing the dawn every morning, so the day could not start and darkness reigned.

The anxious animals assembled to discuss the matter and consulted the guinea fowl, who said, "You have killed my baby; you must first make amends for it, then I will again call in the morning." A court was convened to investigate the events that ended in the smashed egg. The trouble was traced back to the fly's selfish thoughts. The court sentenced the fly to sit for all time with her family on the rubbish behind the house, where you find them to this day.

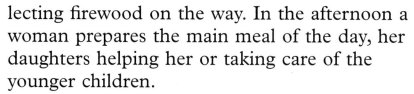

lecting firewood on the way. In the afternoon a woman prepares the main meal of the day, her daughters helping her or taking care of the younger children.

Most men and women do these daily tasks on their own or with family members, but for larger projects—for example, to clean or weed the fields and for harvest—the people organize themselves in groups. They help each other in turn. To work in groups makes the strenuous and tedious work much faster and more pleasant. On some days groups of women go to fish in the larger rivers. In former times hunting was a group activity too, but today the men hunt with only one or two friends.

In the evening the people visit friends or attend a club meeting. Sometimes they just sit in front of the house and chat or tell stories.

▼ ARTS AND CRAFTS ▼

During the dry season there is little farming work and plenty of time for other activities. The family head has a look at the house and discusses with the family members whether it should be repaired or rebuilt. The Ejagham build a house in groups, and help each other in turn. The men construct the scaffold of wooden poles and cover the roof with mats of palm leaves. The women build the walls of clay. In traditional houses

Palm trees are used to create a wide variety of Ejagham products, such as cooking oil, soap, string, mats, and traditional costumes. Ejagham men tap the trunk of a palm tree for palm wine (top), while women prepare palm oil at a local stream (bottom).

most of the interior, including the beds and seats, are made of clay too.

Other projects in the dry season include the repairing of suspension bridges that cross the larger rivers. Men who specialize in wood carving produce drums, statues, masks, or walking sticks. Women make pottery. The Ejagham weave several kinds of mats and bags. Rough mats are used on the floor and to sit on outside; smooth mats with beautiful designs serve as sheets for the beds or as wall decorations.

The women also produce palm oil from palm kernels. First they boil the whole kernels in water. Then they take them in large baskets to the nearby stream where they press the soft outer part of the kernels from which the red oil emerges. From the palm nuts, the women manufacture not only the red oil for cooking, but also soap. The shells are cracked and serve as beads for necklaces or as rattles. The inner part of the nut is ground for body oil. The palm trees themselves are also useful for many different products: sweet palm wine is tapped from the stem; the inner part of the branches provides string; and the ripe leaves are used to weave mats or to cover the roofs, and the fresh green ones are used to decorate masking costumes.▲

chapter

5

RELIGION

RELIGION IS PART OF DAILY LIFE. THE
Ejagham start any activity of importance with a
small prayer to Obasi, the creator, and the ancestors. They do this before every journey, before
going to hunt, when a visitor arrives, before
planning festivities, or when a family member
receives a large present.

On such occasions, the entire family assem-
bles, and the head of the family informs the
ancestors of the event, asks them to support it,
and invites them to take part spiritually in eating
and drinking. The ancestors have to agree to all
important projects. To establish the ancestors'
feelings, the family head performs the ceremony
of throwing the two halves of a kola nut. If both
nuts fall the same way, facing up or down, it is a
sign that the ancestors agree. Otherwise, the
ancestors disapprove, and the people must delay

Ancestors play an important role in Ejagham religion. Above, a family elder stands at the side of a tree commemorating his forefathers.

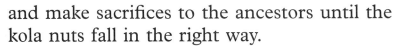

and make sacrifices to the ancestors until the kola nuts fall in the right way.

Besides Obasi and the ancestors, there are minor spirits who reside in special places in the natural environment, such as lakes, rivers, huge trees, and boulders. Finally, there are also the spirits of dead witches and those who died a violent death. They cannot join the ancestors, and therefore they are restless and wander around and disturb people. Offerings are made not only to Obasi and the ancestors, but to appease all these spiritual beings.

Sometimes the spirits can take the shape of an animal or a human being. The python and the crocodile are generally regarded as water spirits in disguise. Certain Ejagham men and women are also said to have this ability, called *efeme*. When you encounter a stranger or a curious animal in the forest, you can never be sure whether the being in front of you is a normal person or animal or a spirit in disguise.

▼ THE ALTAR OF THE WHITE STONES ▼

Most village chiefs have a small altar at the entrance of the community hall. Some family heads have such an altar in a corner of their salon. This is the altar for the *arem*, the nature spirits. From time to time the family head makes an offering at the altar to "feed" the *arem* with red palm oil and corn.

The *arem* have a strong connection with the souls of unborn children. On the altar are two large, shiny, white stones and several small ones. The two big ones represent the parents and remain at the altar the entire time, but the number of smaller stones fluctuates over time. Every time a stone disappears, a woman of the village becomes pregnant; and whenever a new child is born in the village, a small stone appears.

▼ WITCHCRAFT ▼

From time to time the peace of the village is disturbed by the deeds of troublesome, dissatisfied, or envious people. Such people may be called witches or sorcerers. Witchcraft, *oje*, is a power that anybody can use. It can be used to produce extraordinary things that benefit the entire village, but it can also be used to kill people, bring misfortune, and cause accidents.

Njom can be made to serve specific purposes. Seen here is a *njom* for personal protection that protects its owner from evil forces, like witchcraft.

The missionaries often took drastic measures to eliminate Ejagham beliefs. Seen here is a *njom* tree in front of a village community hall that was cut down by missionaries.

The Ejagham have an extraordinary sense of justice and equality. They take great care that nobody troubles anyone else or outdoes others in a way that disadvantages them. When someone experiences a strange event, a series of misfortunes, or deaths in the family, he or she will suspect that a witch is troubling the family.

A troubled person will go to a diviner and ask him to consult his divining chains in order to disempower the witch. The diviner casts the chains and bases his advice on the way the chains fall upon the ground. Often he instructs the client to go to somebody owning a *njom*, a powerful charm, that will protect the client and the client's family and may pursue the witch.

In the center of every village is a major *njom*, which protects the community against witches. Several villagers know the secret of the *njom* and own a part of it, which hangs as a bundle above the entrance to their houses. They sell a small part of it to protect individuals in need against evil and to restore peace in the village.

▼ CHURCHES ▼

When the missionaries came at the beginning of this century to bring Christianity to the Ejagham country, they did not understand well what the Ejagham *njom* were made for. They did not realize that one of their major functions was to protect the people against evil things. They thought the *njom* were tools of the devil and had to be eliminated. In one village a *njom* was cut down by a missionary so that it did not work again. The villagers replaced it after some time, since the church did not solve all their problems. Of course, the church had beneficial influences as well. Today there is a small church in almost every Ejagham village. The Christian church complements the cultural and religious institution of the Ejagham. ▲

At the age of ten, most Ejagham boys enter one of the village boys' clubs, where they practice dancing and other fun group activities. Above, members of a boys' club dance at the New Year's festivities.

chapter

6
CULTURE

FOR A SOCIETY PRACTICING A SUBSISTENCE economy, children are most important. They extend and continue the family and provide extra helping hands in the fields and at home.

The Ejagham are very fond of children. Every baby is welcomed warmly by all the family members and villagers. A few days after its birth, the extended family makes an offering to Obasi and the ancestors to inform them of the event and ask for their help in keeping the baby alive.

▼ MEN'S CLUBS ▼

At approximately age ten a boy usually wants to enter one of the boys' clubs to join his companions of the same age-group. The club is great fun for the boys, and they practice dancing and group activities. Some boys' clubs even own dancing masks.

At the age of fifteen, an Ejagham boy is initiated into the secret club of Angbu. Angbu members must perform several duties, including driving away bad spirits and troublemakers by dancing with their masks (above). Married men from the powerful Ngbe, or leopard club (below), emerge from their secret meeting place in the forest to enforce laws and punish criminals.

When a boy is around fifteen years old, he is initiated into the secret club of Angbu. Angbu is a very serious club, and the young men adhere strictly to its rules. As members of Angbu, the young men perform certain duties for the community, such as watching the entrances of the village or building roads. They also meet to sing and to dance with their masks. The masks of Angbu drive away troublemakers, bad spirits, and witches.

When a man marries, his extended family helps him gain admission and initiation into Ngbe, the men's leopard club, which is very important and powerful. A section in the forest near the village is reserved for the leopard club. Only members are allowed to go there. From time to time the club's masqueraders appear from this sacred forest. They are armed with long whips to enforce laws and punish criminals.

Every man of status must be a member of Ngbe. It is very expensive to enter, since it has many secrets and several grades. To enter each higher grade a man has to pay successively more, gaining in return more of the club's secret knowledge. Only the elders who are in the highest grade of Ngbe know all the secrets. It is a long road to reach the top grade, but once there an elder is highly respected by everybody.

There are other men's clubs, for example, those that own the unique antelope-skin-

These pictures, taken at the turn of the century, illustrate how today's Ejagham traditions are rooted in the past. The figure in the top photograph wears a skin-covered mask for which the Ejagham are famous. Initiates into the famous Ngbogha-Ndem women's club (bottom) learn a secret language and remain highly respected throughout their lives.

covered masks for which the Ejagham are famous. They are the only people in the world who specialized in the complicated technique of producing such masks. Once, all famous hunters and warriors owned skin-covered masks, but today they prefer to cover them with bright industrial paint instead.

▼ GIRLS' INITIATION ▼

There are few clubs for girls. More important for girls is the initiation process, called *monenkim*, which they usually begin when they have given birth to their first child.

The initiation lasts several months—up to a year—during which girls, who would otherwise be doing small jobs to help their mothers, are allowed to rest and practice dancing and singing during most of the day. A girl undergoing initiation has to remain in her father's house, but she may eat as much as she likes. An aunt teaches her songs and shows her how to make the typical Ejagham designs used to ornament the face, body, and objects used in religious ceremonies and daily life. The aunt teaches her to prepare special dishes and reveals the secrets of married life.

As her graduation, the girl gives a big show at a special ceremony. Her parents invite and entertain many guests. To begin the celebration, the leopard club performs. Then the girl performs solo in the village center, surrounded by a large

NSIBIRI: SECRET SIGNS AND WRITING

Nsibiri exists in several forms. Members of the leopard club use it as a secret sign language. It can be used by members, for example, to indicate whether a man of another village is a member too, and how much knowledge he has of the club's secrets. If the other man can't answer in the sign language, it is clear that he has no knowledge of Ngbe and may not participate at the meetings. The knowledge of *nsibiri* is also used to learn the language of the drum.

Nsibiri exists in a written form too. It is mainly used in this way by women. Female initiates learn much of the *nsibiri* writing, including some mimes for the sign language. In former times, initiates painted their faces and the walls of their rooms with *nsibiri* signs. They also decorated large calabashes with *nsibiri*, which were used to collect graduation presents from the spectators for the initiate's parents.

The drawing on the left shows *nsibiri* signs painted on the face of an Ejagham woman. The image on the right is a photograph taken in 1924.

crowd that gathers to watch. While she dances, she sings all the songs she has learned. The women sing as a chorus and the young men play the drums. If the spectators admire her performance, they will give her many presents and ask her to continue. She sometimes performs for several hours.

▼ MARRIAGE ▼

After initiation, a girl generally marries and moves to her husband's house. But her parents will accept the marriage only when the husband has brought a sufficient amount of presents for them.

A marriage is celebrated first in the house of the wife's family. Some days later, a second celebration is held at the house of the husband's family.

In the first months of marriage, the bride's mother-in-law supervises her and takes care of her, teaching her the household routine. Later on, the new wife becomes more independent, planting her own fields and cooking for her husband. Occasionally she visits her parents. Her mother usually encourages her to enter one of the women's clubs, such as Njom Ekpa, the python club.

▼ WOMEN'S CLUBS ▼

A woman enters Njom Ekpa after marriage.

Like the Ejagham men's leopard club, the women's Njom Ekpa, or python club, is very secretive and influential. In the Njom Ekpa performance, seen here, the dancers and the figures in the sculpture all mock men's role in Ejagham society.

The python club is comparable to the men's leopard club and is also very influential. Like the leopard club, it has several grades, secrets, and strong rules. The eldest members know all the club's secrets, which they will never tell a younger woman or a man.

The python club owns a large sculpture, which is danced by one of their expert, younger dancers. The brilliantly colored sculpture consists of a box in which a huge female figure and several smaller figures are placed. Some people call the huge figure Mami Wata; others say it represents a female ancestor. The dancer of this sculpture is accompanied by two girls who carry mirrors. There are also six women dancers who perform men's roles. Each of them is represented in the wooden box by one of the smaller figures. One plays the diviner with his divining chains, another the hunter with his gun, others mime policemen and warriors with large swords, and another plays a foolish warrant chief who tries to interfere everywhere. With this play the women mock men's roles in society. They perform this play at the initiation ceremonies of members, at communal festivities, and at the funeral of a member.

Another famous women's club is called Ngbogha-Ndem. It is one of the clubs that a girl may enter around puberty. The club initiation is similar to that of the *monenkim* club, but much more elaborate. At the end of the initiation, a graduate knows all the secrets of the club and the secret language that only members understand, and she dances for the villagers in a big ceremony. When a member marries, the husband has to give her parents twice as many presents as usual. The members are highly respected throughout their lives. At the funeral of a Ngbogha-Ndem member, a life-size statue, sheltered in a miniature house, is erected in front of her house to remember her. The statue is brightly painted, wears her dancing costume, and sits on a chair, which indicates a high status in Ejagham society. At Ejagham meetings only respected persons are seated.

The Njom Ekpa play is performed at initiation ceremonies, community festivals, and at the funeral of a member. Here, a dancer of the Njom Ekpa mimics a sorcerer.

Funerals are important events in Ejagham cultural life because the dead enter the world of the highly respected ancestors. Seen here is a life-sized grave statue of a Ngbogha-Ndem member placed inside a miniature house. Both are erected outside of a member's home when she dies.

▼ FUNERALS ▼

Funerals are very important in Ejagham cultural life. Some people say that the funeral is the biggest event of one's life. It marks one's entry into the world of the respected ancestors. But only elders and those who are respected by the villagers are honored with a big funeral ceremony.

The seniority of male and female elders lies in their having married, been active members of clubs, and having brought up children who continue the cycle of life. Such elders take part in political decisions, and everybody appreciates

53

Ngbogha-Ndem grave statues are painted in bright colors and wear the member's dancing costume. These grave statues are always seated upon a chair—a position of status at Ejagham village meetings.

their advice and opinions. When such an elder dies, the family of the deceased organizes the festivities. Immediately after the death they prepare a mourning house, hold a small ceremony, and bury the corpse.

However, it is important not only to bury and mourn the deceased, but also to honor him or her. This has to be a big event. Sometimes it takes several years for the family to save enough money to host all the guests and members of the clubs in which the deceased participated. The chief must be a member of all of the village's important clubs. A chief's funeral celebration is therefore one of the biggest festivities in Ejagham country.▲

chapter

7

CITY AND VILLAGE

EJAGHAM SOCIETY AND CULTURE HAVE ALWAYS undergone changes, but in this century they have faced major modifications. Colonization affected the political, economic, and social structures of Ejagham society. It also had a great impact on the ethics and values of the community. Colonial rule and the postcolonial period introduced changes in administration and many foreign goods, but also produced uncertainty about Ejagham identity and their role in the modern states of Cameroon and Nigeria.

▼ WHAT STYLE OF HOUSE? ▼

Houses provide just one example of historical changes. Today most Ejagham save money to build brick houses with corrugated iron roofs. This type of house is more durable than traditional architecture, but it is much more expen-

Today, many small Ejagham towns show Western influences. Above, the town of Buca, in Cameroon, has Western buildings with brick walls and corrugated iron roofs.

sive. In sunny weather it becomes terribly hot inside, whereas traditional houses with palm leaf roofs and clay walls remain comfortably cool and are generally more suitable to the climate.

▼ TRAVELING TO THE CITY ▼

As in most places in the world, the young people in the villages dream of visiting the large city one day. They are well informed about life in the city, about the latest hairstyles, and about designer jeans. They follow the Cameroonian and Nigerian music stars, to whom they listen on their radios and cassette players, or hear playing in the village bars.

Many Ejagham migrated from the villages to

the cities of Cameroon and Nigeria to find jobs and earn more money. Newcomers to the big cities normally have a relative to go to who will try to help them in the beginning. Most of the Ejagham in the towns and cities know each other, often because of the club system.

▼ THE ROLE OF ▼
THE CLUBS

The clubs are another example of adaptation to changes over time. The Ejagham built up their number of clubs over the centuries. Those that were very popular have lasted centuries, others were forgotten. During colonialism, many clubs were abandoned, but others, such as the leopard

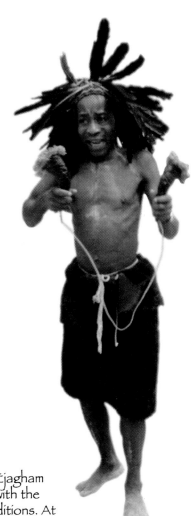

Under colonialism and more recently, many Ejagham clubs were abandoned or, as was the case with the leopard club, were modified to fit the new conditions. At right is Iroko, the messenger of the leopard club.

Ejagham clubs continue to play a positive role in the development of Ejagham country. Club dues or fees now help to pay for the building of roads and improvement of schools and other facilities. Seen here is the market of Buca in Cameroon.

club, were modified to fit the new conditions. Many other clubs were newly invented during this century.

When moving to the cities, the Ejagham took along some of the clubs like Ngbe, which they adapted to the life in the city. They maintain clubs where all the migrated Ejagham can come together and continue the fundamental Ejagham traditions. They have social meetings where they enjoy traditional food, singing, and dancing. The clubs are also a means for spreading news from the villages.

The clubs in the cities and in some of the villages play a positive role in the development of Ejagham country. At each meeting they collect a participation fee. This money is used to

There have been many changes in Ejagham traditions, but their rich artistic heritage continues today. Seen here is a grave statue from the 1920s.

build more schools, install electricity, or even construct roads.

▼ DEVELOPMENT ▼

Due to the changes of this century, some

Ejagham customs come into conflict with other institutions. The Ejagham discuss, for example, to what extent the offerings to the ancestors or polygamy come into conflict with Christian religion, or whether the laws of the ancestors contradict the laws of the state that are influenced by Western legal thinking. They discuss whether young people should continue to do the initiation ceremonies and help their parents in the fields, or whether they should plan for a life lived according to the Western model, requiring fees for a good education in hope of a good job in the city.

Thus the Ejagham constantly adapt, change, and improve their institutions, sustaining a unique and dynamic African culture.▲

Glossary

Angbu Boys' club, entered at around age fifteen.

arem Nature spirits.

etek Village.

mboma Silkcotton tree.

monenkim Girl's initiation process.

ndebe-nju Extended family.

Ngbe Married men's club; the leopard club.

Ngbogha-Ndem Women's club, entered around puberty.

njom Charms.

Njom Ekpa Married women's club; the python club.

nsibiri Secret writing of Ejagham clubs.

ntuifam etek Village chief.

Obasi The Creator.

oje Witchcraft.

okum Social club.

For Further Reading

The few sources that exist on the Ejagham are challenging reading.

Eyongetah, Tambi, and Brain, Robert. *A History of Cameroon*. London: Longman Group Ltd., 1974.

Imoagene, Oshomha. *Peoples of the Cross River Valley and the Eastern Delta*. Ibadan, Nigeria: New Area Educational Company Ltd., 1990.

Talbot, Percy Amaury. *In the Shadow of the Bush*. London: Heineman, 1912.

Willet, Frank. *African Art*. London: Thames & Hudson, 1973.

Index

ABOUT THE AUTHOR
Dr. Ute Maria Röschenthaler was born in southwest Germany. She holds an M.A. in cultural anthropology, literature, and journalism. She received her Ph.D. in cultural anthropology from the Free University of Berlin, Germany, where she now teaches African art. She has also conducted several multicultural and anthropological projects at schools. Her field research among the Ejagham of Cameroon was the basis for her book *Die Kunst der Frauen* (*The Art of Women*) and several publications on the Ejagham, including this volume.

PHOTO CREDITS
Cover and all photos © Ute Röschenthaler, except pp. 46 top, 46 bottom, 48 right, 59, by Alfred Mansfeld, and 48 left, by P. A. Talbot (courtesy of Ute Röschenthaler).

CONSULTING EDITOR
Gary N. van Wyk, Ph.D.

LAYOUT AND DESIGN
Kim Sonsky